WEST CHICAGO PUBLIC LIBRARY DISTRICT

3 6653 00121 6278

P9-CFI-855

West Chicago Public Library District
118 West Washington
West Chicago, IL 60185-2803
Phone # (630) 231-1552

TRICERATOPS

AND OTHER HORNED PLANT-EATERS

Prehistoric World

TRICERATOPS
AND OTHER HORNED PLANT-EATERS

VIRGINIA SCHOMP

BENCHMARK BOOKS

MARSHALL CAVENDISH
NEW YORK

DINOSAURS LIVED MILLIONS OF YEARS AGO. EVERYTHING WE KNOW ABOUT THEM—HOW THEY LOOKED, WALKED, ATE, FOUGHT, MATED, AND RAISED THEIR YOUNG—COMES FROM EDUCATED GUESSES BY THE SCIENTISTS WHO DISCOVER AND STUDY FOSSILS. THE INFORMATION IN THIS BOOK IS BASED ON WHAT MOST SCIENTISTS BELIEVE RIGHT NOW. TOMORROW OR NEXT WEEK OR NEXT YEAR, NEW DISCOVERIES COULD LEAD TO NEW IDEAS. SO KEEP YOUR EYES AND EARS OPEN FOR NEWS FLASHES FROM THE PREHISTORIC WORLD!

With thanks to Dr. Mark A. Norell, Chairman of the Division of Paleontology, American Museum of Natural History, for his expert review of the manuscript.

Benchmark Books
Marshall Cavendish
99 White Plains Road
Tarrytown, New York 10591-9001
www.marshallcavendish.com

© Marshall Cavendish Corporation 2003

All rights reserved.

Library of Congress Cataloging-in-Publication Data

Schomp, Virginia.
Triceratops and other horned plant-eaters / by Virginia Schomp.
    p.cm—Prehistoric world
    Includes index and bibliographical references.
Summary: Describes traits and habits of Triceratops and other dinosaurs that are horned, such as the Chasmosaurus.
ISBN 0-7614-1024-4
1. Triceratops—Juvenile literature. 2. Ceratopsidae—Juvenile literature. [1. Triceratops. 2. Ceratopsians. 3. Dinosaurs.] I. Title.
QE862.O65 S43 2002   567.915′8-dc21   2001049946

Front cover: *Triceratops*   Back cover: *Einiosaurus*   Page 2 (left to right): *Triceratops, Pachyrhinosaurus, Styracosaurus*

Photo Credits:
Cover illustration: Marshall Cavendish Corporation

The illustrations and photographs in this book are used by the permission and through the courtesy of:
Marshall Cavendish Corporation: 10, 11, 12, 13, 14, 17, 18, 19, 20, 21, 22, 23, 24, back cover. *The Natural History Museum, London:* Orbis, 8; John Sibbick, 2, 15. *Photo Researchers, Inc.:* Francois Gohier, 25.

Map and Dinosaur Family Tree by Robert Romagnoli

Printed in Hong Kong
1 3 5 6 4 2

For Krysten and Will

Contents

The charge of a horned dinosaur must have been an alarming sight. Like a modern-day rhinoceros, this dinosaur probably could run short distances at surprising speeds.

THE "HORNED FACES"

Angry cries shake the forest. Two horned dinosaurs are fighting. One is a tough old bull covered with battle scars, the leader of the herd grazing among the trees. The other is a young male, slightly smaller but strong. Snorting and grunting, the pair paw the ground. They shake their heads, waving their long horns and giant neck frills. Suddenly the young dinosaur charges. Locking horns, the fighters push and twist, each straining to knock the other off balance. At last the older bull breaks away, exhausted. Chasing its rival into the forest, the young male dinosaur bellows in triumph. Then it takes its place as the herd's new leader.

With its massive horns and neck frill, *Triceratops* was one of the oddest-looking animals ever to walk the earth. It was also one of the very last dinosaurs. Sixty-five million years ago, at the end of the Age of Dinosaurs, this mighty marvel was still going strong in the plains and forests of North America.

The Age of Dinosaurs

Dinosaurs walked the earth during the Mesozoic era, also known as the Age of Dinosaurs. The Mesozoic era lasted from about 250 million to 65 million years ago. It is divided into three periods: the Triassic, Jurassic, and Cretaceous.

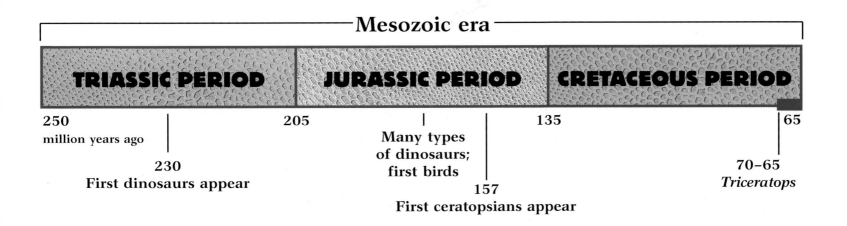

FRILLY COUSINS

Imagine a family picnic where everyone munches on trees and wears five-foot-tall party hats. A gathering of *Triceratops*'s relatives might seem just as bizarre. *Triceratops* belonged to a group of dinosaurs called ceratopsians, or "horned faces." Ceratopsians were plant-eaters that lived in North America and Asia from 157 million to 65 million years ago. Most ceratopsians had horns on their heads and tall, fancy neck frills.

Triceratops

Styracosaurus

Protoceratops

Microceratops

Ceratopsians came in many sizes and varieties—from tiny Microceratops *all the way to mighty horned* Triceratops.

CENTROSAURUS
(sen-troh-SORE-us)
When: Late Cretaceous,
80–70 million years ago
Where: Alberta, Canada
* Long nose horn;
  2 small brow horns
* Lived in large herds

A ceratopsian's neck frill was used for defense and for attracting a mate, and may also have kept the dinosaur cool and helped hold its heavy jaw muscles. Some ceratopsians, like this Centrosaurus, *may have had brightly colored frills.*

A horned dinosaur's frill was made of bone growing from the back of its skull. *Triceratops* and its cousins probably showed off their bony collars to attract mates. They may also have used their neck frills to scare away enemies. Ducking their heads and waving their frills, they tried to make themselves look even bigger and more dangerous.

Most ceratopsians were built like overgrown rhinoceroses—big, heavy, and well armed. Some had short neck frills and long nose horns. Others had longer frills and shorter nose horns. *Triceratops* was the largest and heaviest of the long-frilled group. The chart on page 26 shows how this jumbo plant-eater and its ceratopsian cousins fit into the dinosaur family tree.

BRACHYCERATOPS
(brack-ee-SAIR-uh-tops)
When: Late Cretaceous,
80–70 million years ago
Where: Montana
◆ Long nose horn;
  2 short brow horns
◆ Weighed about as much
  as 2 white rhinoceroses

Scientists group large ceratopsians by the size of their neck frills. Brachyceratops belonged to the short-frilled group . . .

. . . and Anchiceratops was a long-frilled ceratopsian.

ANCHICERATOPS
(ang-kih-SAIR-uh-tops)
When: Late Cretaceous,
80–70 million years ago
Where: Canada
◆ Large frill decorated
  with triangular horns
◆ Short nose horn;
  2 long curved brow horns

TRICERATOPS
(try-SAIR-uh-tops)
When: Late Cretaceous,
70–65 million years ago
Where: North America
* 25 to 30 feet long;
  9 feet high at the hip
* Weighed 5 tons

A powerful Triceratops *uses its huge head like a battering ram to knock over a tree, so it can get to the juicy leaves and twigs at the top.*

THREE-HORNED GIANT

As long as two cars. Heavier than an African elephant. *Triceratops* packed all that bulk into a barrel-shaped body with four sturdy legs and a long, muscular tail. The most impressive part of this powerful beast's body was its enormous head. Stretching more than six feet, *Triceratops*'s head took up nearly a third of its body length. The broad frill growing from the back of its skull was a solid slab of bone.

Triceratops means "three-horn face." Three horns sprouted from this dinosaur's massive head—one on its nose and two above its eyes. The brow horns were more than three feet long and ended in a sharp point. They were powerful weapons for protection from the dangerous predators that shared this horned giant's world.

THE NAME GAME

Why do dinosaurs have such weird-looking, tongue-twisting names? Believe it or not, it's to make them easier to talk about and study.

When a new kind of dinosaur is discovered, it is often given a name made up of a combination of Greek or Latin words. These languages are recognized by scientists all over the world, so no matter where they live, all scientists call the dinosaur by the same name. That name may describe something about the dinosaur's body or behavior, or it may honor the place where it was found or the person who found it.

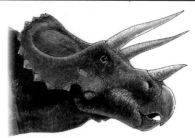

tri (three) + *keratos* (horn) + *ops* (face) =
Triceratops

velox (swift) + *raptor* (robber) =
Velociraptor

Argentino (discovered in Argentina) + *sauros** (lizard) =
Argentinosaurus

Lambe (discovered by Lawrence Lambe) + *sauros** (lizard) =
Lambeosaurus

*Many dinosaur names end in saurus. *These amazing animals weren't really lizards, but the name given them in 1841 has stuck anyway:* deinos *("fearfully great" or "terrible")* + saurus *("lizard")* = dinosaur.

Evergreen trees, shrubs, ferns, and moss made the Cretaceous world a vast green garden, filled with food for Triceratops *and other hungry plant-eaters.*

WORLD BEFORE TIME

Can you imagine a world without people? Without houses and factories, roads and cars? Let's journey back to that world. Back some sixty-five million years, to Late Cretaceous North America—the home of *Triceratops*.

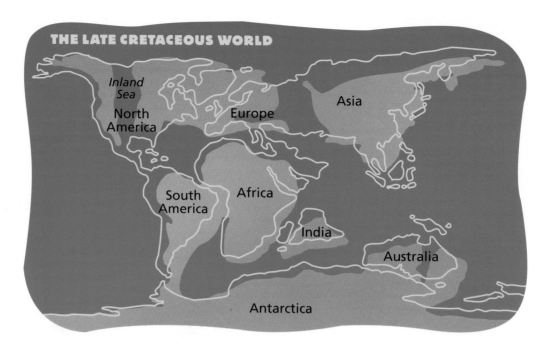

THE LATE CRETACEOUS WORLD

The yellow outlines on this map show the shape of the modern continents. The green shading shows their position around sixty-five million years ago, in the days of Triceratops.

TROUBLE IN PARADISE

Our time machine lands in a world as warm and steamy as a greenhouse. We step out into a lush green meadow dotted with tiny points of color—the world's first flowering plants began to appear early in Cretaceous times. In the distance stands a thick evergreen forest. Beyond the trees, a warm sea sparkles.

At the beginning of the Age of Dinosaurs, the earth had one huge super-continent surrounded by a giant sea. Over time that landmass broke up, and the pieces drifted to form the continents we know today. Water poured in to fill the gaps, forming new seas. In the Late Cretaceous period, one vast body of water reaches from the top to the bottom of North America, separating west from east.

A crocodile makes a meal of a young Albertosaurus. *Crocodiles first appeared about two hundred million years ago and were abundant in the Cretaceous period.*

Many different animals live in this wild, wet paradise. Some are familiar to us—crocodiles, lizards, turtles, small mammals, birds. But it is the amazing, alien-looking dinosaurs that dominate. Duck-billed dinosaurs gobble up the flowers. Horned dinosaurs roam the landscape. Trailing all these plant-eaters are some of the most dangerous predators the world has ever known. We shiver at the sight of sharp-fanged *Albertosaurus*. And when we hear the roar of the king of killers, *Tyrannosaurus*, we might decide it's time to return to our own tame world.

EINIOSAURUS
(eye-nee-oh-SORE-us)
When: Late Cretaceous,
  80–70 million years ago
Where: Montana
◆ Large forward-curved nose
  horn
◆ Short frill with 2 long spikes

Bones from a herd of hundreds of Einiosaurus *have been discovered buried together; the dinosaurs may have died of thirst or while trying to cross a swift river.*

LIFE IN THE HERD

Triceratops was built for defense. Its giant frill shielded its neck and back from teeth and claws, and its three curved horns were lethal weapons. If a predator attacked, *Triceratops* might have stood its ground, shaking its head and roaring a warning. Or it might have pointed its horns and charged. This five-ton giant could move surprisingly fast when it had to—perhaps up to twenty-five miles an hour for short distances.

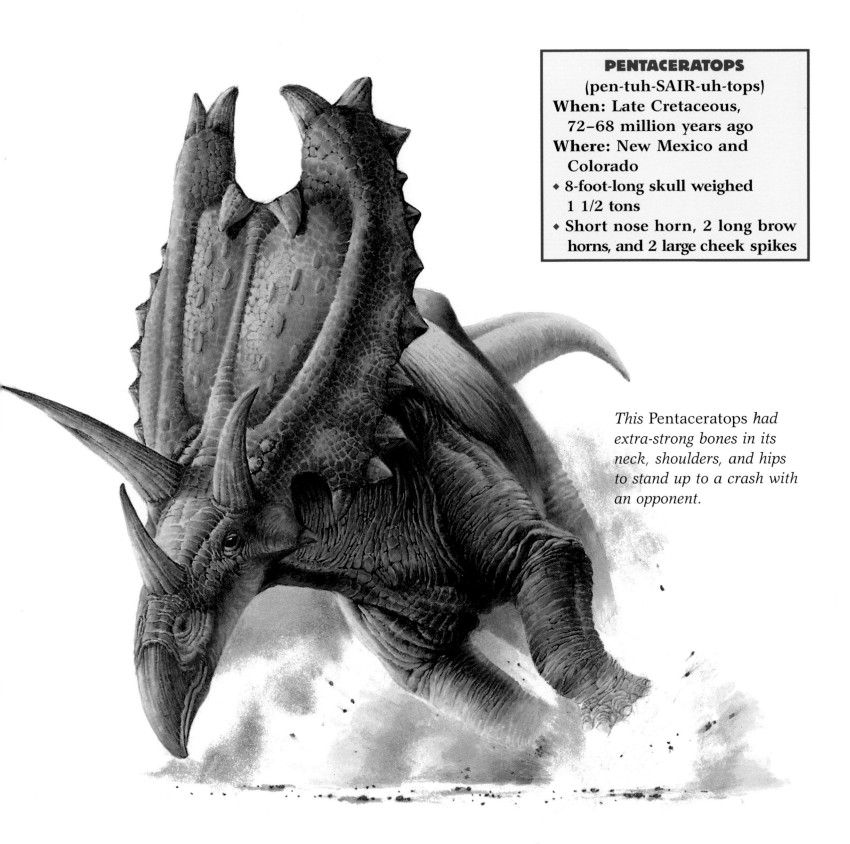

PENTACERATOPS
(pen-tuh-SAIR-uh-tops)
When: Late Cretaceous,
72–68 million years ago
Where: New Mexico and
Colorado
- 8-foot-long skull weighed
  1 1/2 tons
- Short nose horn, 2 long brow
  horns, and 2 large cheek spikes

This Pentaceratops *had
extra-strong bones in its
neck, shoulders, and hips
to stand up to a crash with
an opponent.*

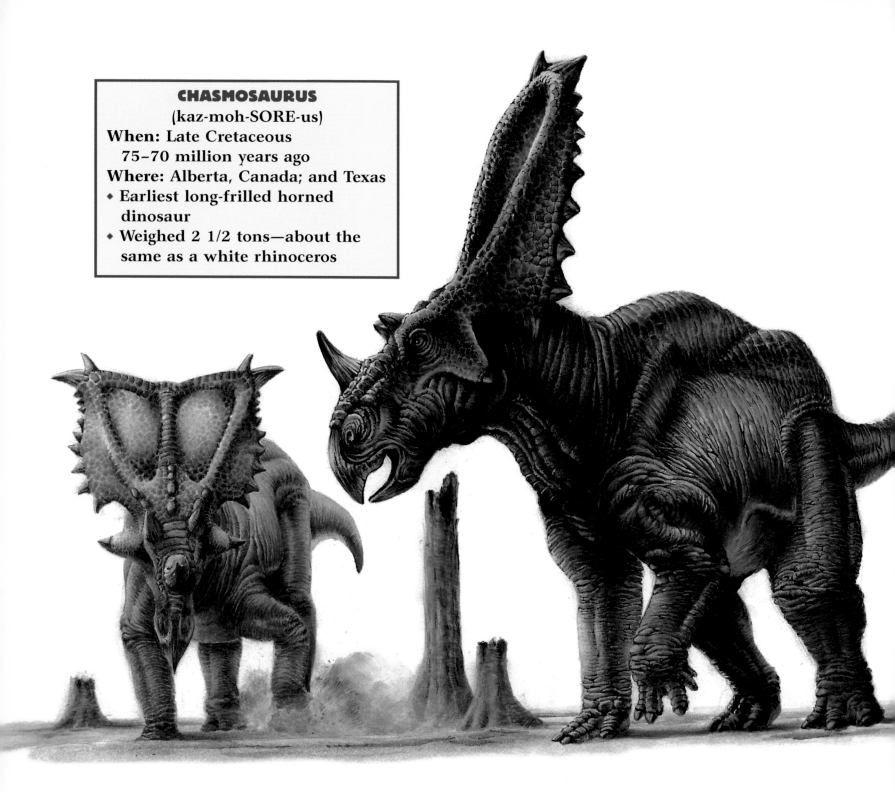

CHASMOSAURUS
(kaz-moh-SORE-us)
When: Late Cretaceous
75–70 million years ago
Where: Alberta, Canada; and Texas
◆ Earliest long-frilled horned
dinosaur
◆ Weighed 2 1/2 tons—about the
same as a white rhinoceros

These fearsome horned dinosaurs might be competing for a mate or for feeding grounds, or to decide which one will lead the herd.

Little Leptoceratops *had powerful jaws and a sharp parrotlike beak designed to cut through even the toughest plants.*

LEPTOCERATOPS
(lep-toh-SAIR-uh-tops)
When: Late Cretaceous,
  70–65 million years ago
Where: Alberta, Canada;
  and Wyoming
◆ Small, primitive ceratopsian with
  no horns and a small neck frill
◆ Ran fast on two legs or all fours

SAFETY IN NUMBERS

For extra protection, *Triceratops* may have lived in large groups, or herds. Most of the time, these hungry herders tramped through the plains and forests of North America in search of food. Their sharp, curved beaks clipped off mouthfuls of low-growing twigs and leaves, which they shredded to a pulp with their scissorlike cheek teeth.

The herd's constant munching was occasionally interrupted by combat. Waggling their neck frills and sometimes locking horns, male *Triceratops* challenged each other to battle. Only the strongest got a chance to lead the herd and mate with the females.

DEADLY RING

Like all dinosaurs, baby *Triceratops* hatched from eggs. No one knows how horned dinosaurs cared for their babies, but some scientists think that young and old lived together in the herds. When a hungry predator threatened, the adults may have taken charge. Pushing the youngsters behind them, they formed a protective circle. Facing that ring of raised frills and sharp horns, most predators probably gave up on fresh *Triceratops* steak and stalked off in search of an easier meal.

ARRHINOCERATOPS
(ah-rie-no-SAIR-uh-tops)
When: Late Cretaceous,
  75–70 million years ago
Where: Alberta, Canada
• Short face and neck frill
• Small nose horn; 2 outward-
  curved brow horns

One Arrhinoceratops *skull discovered by fossil hunters had a hole in its frill—probably an injury suffered in a sparring contest with another horned male.*

STYRACOSAURUS
(stie-rack-uh-SORE-us)
When: Late Cretaceous,
  75–70 million years ago
Where: Montana and Canada
• Nose horn nearly 2 feet long
• Short frill with 6 long spikes
  and several shorter ones

Few predators would dare to attack a herd of fierce-looking Styracosaurus. *The spikes on this ceratopsian's delicate frill were mainly for show, but its sharp nose horn could do plenty of damage.*

Ash from a distant volcano turns the sky red above a herd of horned dinosaurs. Some scientists think the dinosaurs became extinct because of erupting volcanoes or falling sea levels, while others say they died after a giant asteroid crashed into the earth.

Triceratops *bones have been discovered all over North America, preserved for millions of years as fossils.*

AN UNSOLVED MYSTERY

Extinction is a part of life on earth. Over time different kinds of animals appear and die out. Sometimes many kinds of animals become extinct at once. That happened sixty-five million years ago, when all the dinosaurs disappeared. Paleontologists—scientists who study prehistoric life—have different ideas about what may have caused this mass extinction. The final answer remains a mystery.

Triceratops was one of the last living dinosaurs. It left behind hundreds of fossils—hardened bones and other remains. By studying these long-buried treasures, paleontologists gather clues about this amazing three-horned giant and life in the final days of the dinosaurs.

Dinosaur Family Tree

ORDER

All dinosaurs are divided into two large groups, based on the shape and position of their hipbones. Ornithischians had backward-pointing hipbones.

SUBORDER

Marginocephalians were plant-eating dinosaurs with a narrow shelf or deep bony frill at the back of the skull.

INFRAORDER

Ceratopsians had bony neck frills and horns.

FAMILY

A family includes one or more types of closely related dinosaurs.

GENUS

Every dinosaur has a two-word name. The first word tells us what genus, or type, of dinosaur it is. The genus plus the second word is its species— the group of very similar animals it belongs to. (For example, *Triceratops horridus* is one species of *Triceratops*.)

Scientists organize all living things into groups, according to features shared.
This chart shows the groupings of the horned plant-eaters in this book.

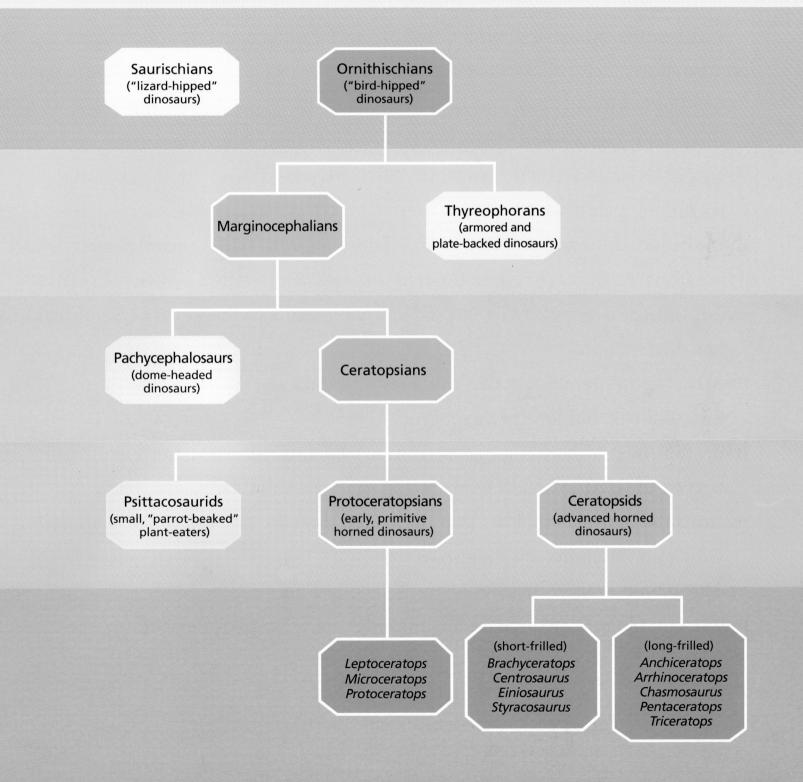

Glossary

Albertosaurus: one of North America's most common tyrannosaurs (two-fingered meat-eating dinosaurs), which lived from 80 million to 68 million years ago

ceratopsians (seh-ruh-TOPE-see-yuns): a group of plant-eating dinosaurs that lived in North America and Asia from about 157 million to 65 million years ago; most ceratopsians had sharp beaks, horns on their heads, and bony neck frills

Cretaceous (krih-TAY-shus) **period:** the time period from about 135 million to 65 million years ago

duck-billed dinosaurs: plant-eating dinosaurs with wide, shovel-shaped beaks, which were the most common land animals of the Late Cretaceous period

extinction: the act of dying out; an animal is extinct when every one of its kind has died

fossils: the hardened remains or traces of animals or plants that lived many thousands or millions of years ago

frill: the sheet of bone that grew from the back of a ceratopsian's skull and curved upward to shield its neck and often its shoulders

mammals: animals that are warm-blooded, breathe air, and nurse their young with milk; humans are mammals

predator: an animal that hunts and kills other animals for food

primitive: simple or basic; belonging to an early stage of development

Find Out More

BOOKS

Cohen, Daniel. *Triceratops and Other Cretaceous Plant-Eaters.* Minneapolis: Capstone, 1996.

The Humongous Book of Dinosaurs. New York: Stewart, Tabori, and Chang, 1997.

Lindsay, William. *Triceratops: On the Trail of the Incredible Armored Dinosaur.* New York: Dorling Kindersley, 1993.

Marshall, Chris, ed. *Dinosaurs of the World.* 11 vols. New York: Marshall Cavendish, 1999.

Parker, Steve. *The Age of the Dinosaurs.* Vol. 11, *The Ceratopsians.* Danbury, CT: Grolier Educational, 2000.

Vaughan, Jenny. *Looking at Triceratops.* Milwaukee: Gareth Stevens, 1993.

ON-LINE SOURCES *

***Dino Russ's Lair: Dinosaur and Vertebrate Paleontology Information* at**
http://www.isgs.uiuc.edu/dinos/dinos_home.html

Created by geologist Russ Jacobson, this website includes a very useful collection of links to museums and other organizations that provide on-line information about dinosaurs.

***University of California, Berkeley, Museum of Paleontology* at**
http://www.ucmp.berkeley.edu

This site has lots of information and photos, but it can be a bit difficult to navigate; your best bet is to use the site's Search engine to zero in on a term (for example, type in "Dinosaurs" or "Triceratops").

***UW Geological Museum Tour* at**
http://www.uwyo.edu/geomuseum/Tour.htm

Tour the University of Wyoming Geological Museum, where a special exhibit honors Wyoming's official state dinosaur, *Triceratops*.

***Zoom Dinosaurs* at http://www.zoomdinosaurs.com**

This colorful, entertaining site from Enchanted Learning Software includes a world of information on dinosaur-related topics: dinosaur myths, records, behavior, and fossils; dinosaur fact sheets; quizzes, puzzles, printouts, and crafts; tips on writing a school report; and more.

Website addresses sometimes change. For more on-line sources, check with the media specialist at your local library.

Index

Virginia Schomp grew up in a quiet suburban town in northeastern New Jersey, where eight-ton duck-billed dinosaurs once roamed. In first grade she discovered that she loved books and writing, and in sixth grade she was named "class bookworm," because she always had her nose in a book. Today she is a freelance author who has written more than thirty books for young readers on topics including careers, animals, ancient cultures, and modern history. Ms. Schomp lives in the Catskill Mountain region of New York with her husband, Richard, and their son, Chip.